THE
CUSTO

HUNGARY

ABOUT THE AUTHOR

LÁSZLÓ JOTISCHKY was born and educated in Hungary, but
has lived in London since 1956. He used to work in the BBC
World Service where he headed the Hungarian Section for
five years. He is currently a freelance broadcaster and
journalist and the London correspondent of the Budapest daily
Új Magyarország.

ILLUSTRATED BY
PETER SEARLE

THE SIMPLE GUIDE TO CUSTOMS AND ETIQUETTE IN

HUNGARY

LÁSZLÓ JOTISCHKY

GLOBAL BOOKS LTD

Simple Guides • Series 1
CUSTOMS & ETIQUETTE

The Simple Guide to
CUSTOMS & ETIQUETTE IN HUNGARY
by László Jotischky

First published 1995 by
GLOBAL BOOKS LTD
PO Box 219, Folkestone, Kent, England CT20 3LZ

ISBN 1–86034–035–0

British Library Cataloguing in Publication Data
A CIP catalogue entry for this book
is available from the British Library

Distributed in the USA & Canada by:
The Talman Co. Inc
131 Spring Street
New York, NY 10012
USA

Set in Futura 11 on 12 pt by Bookman, Slough
Printed in Great Britain by
The Cromwell Press, Broughton Gifford, Wiltshire

Contents

Foreword

The two key points to understanding Hungarians and their ways are their mainly Germanic and Slavic neighbours, and the fact that, in 1990, they found themselves free from foreign military occupation and Communist dictatorship which had lasted for more than 40 years.

Under the circumstances of the late 1980s and early 1990s, it was easier to achieve national independence and individual freedom than to reap the political, moral and economic benefits of these achievements. National independence brought with it the urgent need of a foreign policy which provides good relations with immediate neighbours whose sentiments towards Hungary and Hungarians are less than favourable.

Translating freedom into everyday practice without chaos demanded immediate and sound legislation as well as the responsible co-operation of individuals as members of a civil society. After the devastating effects of Soviet-type socialism and crippling foreign indebtedness, the national economy seemed to defy efforts towards improvement.

Five years of freedom have failed to match Western freedom with Western affluence, and Hungarians are angry, bewildered and disillusioned.

L.J.
Spring 1995

1

Introducing Hungary

Parliament building from the Danube

The forebears of present-day Hungarians were carried into the Danube valley (Carpathian Basin) around what is now Budapest on the tide of the great westward migration of peoples in the early Middle Ages. By the end of the ninth century they had defeated, and had begun to assimilate, the peoples that had previously settled the area and King Stephen I (1001–1031) was able to establish a nation-state and to convert the many pagan and few Eastern-rite Christian Hungarians to Western Catholicism, thereby irreversibly tying them to the West.

The history of the Hungarians has been determined by two principal factors: their geographic position on the East-West highway of Europe among ethnically alien neighbours,

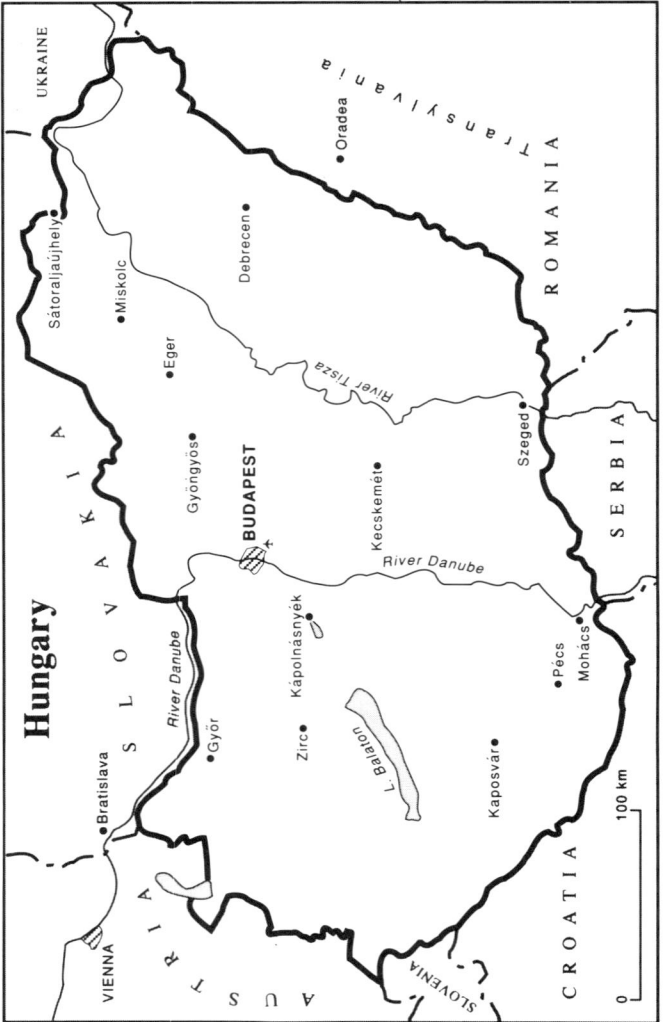

Hungary

UKRAINE

SLOVAKIA

Bratislava

VIENNA

AUSTRIA

SLOVENIA

CROATIA

SERBIA

ROMANIA

Transylvania

River Danube

River Danube

River Tisza

•Sátoraljaújhely

•Miskolc

•Eger

•Gyöngyös

•Oradea

•Debrecen

BUDAPEST

Kecskemét•

Szeged•

Zirc•

•Győr

Kápolnásnyék•

L. Balaton

Kaposvár•

•Pécs

Mohács•

100 km

0

and their relatively small number. There were not enough Hungarians to populate the Carpathian Basin completely, and, in fighting against German expansion in the form of Hapsburg colonization in the West, and invading Mongols and Turks in the East, the numbers could never grow significantly.

When the country, after 300 years of wars and 150 years of actual Turkish occupation, finally found itself free from the Ottoman Empire it was too exhausted to resist Austria's colonial expansion under the Hapsburg dynasty.

Although between the end of the seventeenth and the middle of the nineteenth century three full-scale wars of independence were fought and suppressed, Hungary was ruled more or less as a Hapsburg crown colony until 1867. It was then that, seizing the opportunity provided by a series of Austrian military reverses, Hungarian politicians successfully negotiated special status for Hungary among the many Hapsburg dependencies.

Franz Joseph was crowned King of Hungary and the country became junior partner in what became known as the Austro-Hungarian Empire, within which Hungary governed itself with the exception of foreign, fiscal and defence policy, and a number of Hungarian politicians attained a leading role in the government of the whole Empire.

The 1919 Versailles Peace Treaty at the end of the First World War, dismembered the Empire and, in the process, granted two-thirds of historical Hungary to its neighbours. Hungarian foreign policy between the World Wars was dominated by the desire to regain as much of the loss as possible. This placed Hungary on the side of Germany and the Axis Powers during the Second World War and resulted in yet another defeat and dismemberment at the Paris Peace Treaty of 1947.

Today, there are about 15 million Hungarians in the world and every third one of them lives outside the national borders. This does not make for an easy relationship with neighbours and helps to foster the self-pity which has, over the centuries, become an understandable but unattractive feature of the collective Hungarian psyche.

The Hungarian emblem

Two of the country's national days mark national uprisings: 15 March commemorates the start of the last War of Independence against the Hapsburgs in 1848, and 23 October was the day in 1956 when a popular uprising swept away the communist state until, 12 days later, Soviet tanks restored it; 6 October is a day of mourning for the martyrs of these two uprisings. Only one national day, 20 August (St Stephen's Day) marks a lasting success: the canonized King Stephen's achievement in putting a new nation on the map of Europe. The country's coat of arms is based on that of his dynasty and the crown on it is his crown, sent to him by Pope Sylvester II (believed to be essentially the same as the one exhibited in the National Museum in Budapest).

A relic, alleged to be King Stephen's right hand, is exhibited in the Basilica of St Stephen in Budapest. Another national shrine is Heroes' Square, with statuary representing the seven chieftains of the conquering Hungarian tribes, as well as kings and heroes of the nation. The tomb of the Unknown Soldier is in the middle of the Square, also dedicated to the fallen freedom fighters of 1956.

2

Meeting Hungarians

Galéria Bar, Mihály Vitkovies Street

The foreign, especially Western, visitor usually finds Hungarians friendly, helpful and hospitable. This is not necessarily how they see themselves, but this is the image they like to present to the outsider whom they wish to impress.

The clue to the collective Hungarian mind is isolation. This may be the last word you would use for the condition of a country with wide-open, indeed indefensible borders, an annual influx of foreign visitors that far exceeds its own population, and who as a people are passionate travellers themselves.

However, the sense of isolation is deeper and has two main causes. One is the linguistic and, to some extent, cultural uniqueness of the nation. It speaks and lovingly cultivates a language that has given birth to many centuries of valuable, in some instances great literature, which cannot be enjoyed by any but the 10.5 million Hungarians who live in Hungary and by the other five million who do not.

This is the second source of the isolation feeling. Hungarians, because of their history, have mostly felt abandoned by the outside world. The fact that, after the Versailles peace treaty, much of the original territory of the ancient Hungarian Kingdom ended up within the national frontiers of neighbouring countries that had only recently emerged as nation states, did nothing to dispel the feeling of being friendless and isolated.

These experiences have produced a sense of insecurity, and also of superiority which, in turn, tend to compel the hosts to demonstrate to their visitors a higher standard of culture, of living style and of hospitality than they could expect elsewhere in the region. That this should favour visitors from the West, rather than the East, is only natural as they are the ones whose own standards are admired and emulated.

The illuminated capital 'S' of King Istvan
from an illustrated Chronicle of 1358

Hungarians, like most East Europeans, for a long time tended to like the West because they had been suppressed by their powerful and overbearing Eastern neighbours, and because the West was constantly and unthinkingly slandered by the Communist authorities. It must be said, though, that five years of experience, partly through contacts with Western business and visitors, have gone some way towards changing this rosy, and altogether unrealistic picture.

Expectations of Western help had been too high while Western aid programmes often proved to be little more than visits from foreigners who, with little or no knowledge of local circumstances, were dispensing more advice than dollars. Hence, while the reception extended to Western business people is unlikely to be less than friendly, an element of suspicion will prevail.

Hungarian hospitality is often expressed with gifts such as pieces of folk art, books on Hungary, or typical Hungarian foodstuffs. There is an assumption that Western visitors (thought to be affluent) will reciprocate. In any event, an exchange of gifts is seen as a matter of politeness.

The Hungarian sense of humour is keen and ready to erupt regardless of any language problems! Sometimes it can be extremely irritating when long and elaborate anecdotes have to be endured without there being any obvious point. Also, a lack of appreciation for bawdy humour, especially on the part of men, is simply seen as unfriendly.

On the other hand, some things are taken too seriously, such as invitations. Do not extend vague invites like 'You must really come

and see us when you are in . . . (your country)'
if you do not actually mean it; do not say 'Why
don't you come around for a drink one evening'
if you do not want to be asked which evening
and what time. Nor is it good enough to say 'I
shall come and see you sometime' unless you
mean to do so. Joviality in social intercourse
must not be mistaken for casualness, and it must
always be remembered that personal friend-
ship with a Westerner is still considered to be
an asset.

If you are brave enough to have a go at the
Hungarian language (see Chapter 10) and
wish to address new acquaintances in their
own tongue, remember that the familiar second
person singular (**te**) and the corresponding verb
forms are, more or less as in French, German
and many other languages, reserved for close
friends and colleagues, or members of the
family. Indeed, many Hungarians of the older
generation still address their parents and other
older relatives in the more polite third person
(e.g. '**Hogy van, édesanyám?**' = '*How is
mother?*'). Using the familiar form where it is
improper will earn the foreigner good-natured
laughter and correction, at best.

Oldest known woodcut (1470) of Buda

The familiar form, however, is spreading fast among the young (up to, say, 25) and the young visitor will not be embarrassed by using the familiar form as long as the Hungarian partner is of a similar age and the same sex.

Another potential source of embarrassment is the use of the greeting (and farewell) **kezicsókolom** or, more simply **csókolom**. This is a corruption of **kezét csókolom**, meaning '*I kiss your hand*'. This is acceptable from any child in every situation, and from any male of any age when said to any female above schoolgirl age. Very young women may also greet their obvious female elders this way, or adults of either sex their relatives of an older generation, or their parents' friends. However, barring older relatives or family friends, nobody can greet men this way without courting ridicule.

You may find it surprising, especially if you are not a regular visitor to Germany or Austria where a similar situation prevails, how many Hungarians have the title 'Dr'. In Hungary all men and women with a degree from a medical school are called doctor. A Hungarian surgeon would feel insulted if addressed as 'Mr'. Also, all graduates of law faculties, with a law degree, are titled as doctor and normally addressed as such.

Finally, as the acquisition of a doctor's degree in the Hungarian academic system is hardly more demanding than that of an M.A. degree in Britain or the USA, a considerable number of economists, teachers, chemists, engineering graduates and others hold the title. Upon first meeting, it is impolite to ignore it, if you see Dr on the person's visiting card, in the telephone book, or on the name plate on his front door.

A curious rule of polite intercourse is that the way to address people of professional qualifications in Hungarian, at first meeting (even on social occasions) is not 'Mr' followed by the name, but 'Mr' followed by the professional title, rather like 'Mr President'. a TV interviewer would not address a government minister as 'Mr X', but as 'Mr Minister'. Similarly, upon introduction at a dinner party to a man who is a schoolmaster, it is less polite to address him as 'Mr Y' than 'Master' (**Tanár úr** = 'Mr Teacher').

A 'bone-cracking grip'

On meeting Hungarians, remember the Continental habit of shaking hands on every occasion. This is customary not only on introduction. Hungarians believe in a hearty, sincere handshake and even a diminutive, romantic-looking young lady may produce a surprisingly steely, bone-cracking grip!

For the reasons given earlier, Hungarians who may shamelessly knock things Hungarian themselves, do not take kindly to being told that the visitor has formed a bad impression of their country. If anything, Hungarians tend to be overly touchy on the topic of Hungary. Their patriotism was formed by a long history of real and imagined hurts and they react to these with pride in their real and imaginary achievements.

Hungarians will not, therefore, expect the foreign visitor to inform them that the air in Budapest is foul and many of its buildings want a thorough scrubbing if not a major overhaul, that Hungarian food is too rich or too spicy and that it is a major nuisance to walk in narrow streets where the pavements are almost totally taken over by parked cars. Instead, they want to hear that Budapest presents a spectacular panorama to the visitor, that Hungarian food is delicious and that Hungary has nearly as many cars in proportion of its population as the United States.

One good and reasonably safe way of satisfying this hunger for international approbation without compromising one's own integrity, is to congratulate your hosts upon Hungary's prowess in sports. People who would be in serious danger of drowning in anything deeper than a bathtub will smile with conceit if the glory of Hungary's swimmers in the 1992 Olympics in Barcelona is mentioned, and rotund elderly gentlemen who have never kicked a ball towards a goal, will bemoan the present unsatisfactory state of Hungarian football, but will not allow you to forget that, in 1953, a Hungarian side beat England 6:3 at Wembley.

Although not impolite, it is unwise to tackle Hungarians on their domestic politics. Before the fall of Communism, the simple rule was not to embarrass officials with anti-regime remarks or pointed questions because they agreed with you but could not say so. Private contacts would not need much encouragement from you to give vent to their anti-regime sentiments.

Today's situation, however, is more complex. Democracy has brought a multi-party system with it (see Chapter 9) and people have become partisan. The careless visitor might expose himself to long harangues against a government which is depicted in the most lurid colours as incompetent and dishonest, or, just as easily, to a lecture on the opposition as being unpatriotic and destructive. The only thing an innocent visitor can do in a situation like this, is to smile, make abusive remarks about the government (or opposition) of his or her own country and claim diplomatic immunity from Hungary's inner strife – the new national pastime!

Károly Gardens, Budapest

3

At Home

Art Nouveau on Lajos Kossuth Street

Do not be surprised if a Hungarian, no matter how friendly, does not invite you to his home; the fact is, he may not have one. Home construction was neglected in Hungary during most of the Communist years, so it is common for newlyweds to move in with parents, even grandparents, nor is it outrageous for three adult generations to share a four-room flat!

Most urban Hungarians are flat dwellers and most flats are rented. Blocks of flats, especially the older ones, tend to be in sad need of repair. It is not rare for the visitor to ascend badly lit stairs between walls in need of a pot of paint, to find himself in Aladdin's cave, resplendent with antique furniture, oil paintings and Persian carpets. Tenants do not spend on the house, only on their home.

Hungarians are house-proud and a lot of money as well as somewhat old-fashioned good taste is spent on their homes. Visitors are expected to express appropriate interest and admiration!

The typical urban Hungarian home is a flat, all on one level, with considerably less living space, and certainly fewer rooms, than the typical family house in Britain or North America. Not surprisingly, therefore, few Hungarian households, especially in towns, can offer overnight hospitality. Guest rooms are rare, while a second bathroom is a real luxury!

Unlike in most cities in the Western world, the address is rarely an indication of the family's socio-economic standing. To be sure, a brand new, or expensively converted or reconstructed villa in the Buda hills indicates a lot of money behind it. Yet, owing to the devastation of World War II, the influx of people – especially factory workers – into the

Opening of horse-drawn railway 1866

capital during the late 1940s and early 1950s and, in no small measure, to the deliberate housing policy of the Communist regime in the first half of the 1950s, almost all large flats were divided between two or more families. Working-class families were moved into formerly exclusively elegant districts and new council housing was built in the middle of areas where, earlier, almost all buildings used to be family houses and villas.

Visitors to Budapest from cities which largely conform with the British and North American urban pattern of living may also be surprised to find that the majority of people live, literally, above the shop —except not their own shops. Most blocks of flats, especially the ones built before the last war, accommodate shops and other businesses as well. Budapest, therefore, has no typical 'business' or 'downtown' area with relatively few homes, and very few suburban 'dormitory' areas (mainly in the hills of Buda) where few buildings have shops or other businesses in them.

The Hungarian home is hardly a smokeless zone and the visitor need not be shy about his or her smoking habits, at least as far as cigarettes are concerned. (Pipes may be a different matter.)

The ideal present to a hostess from a dinner guest is a bunch of flowers. While dinner jackets are never worn for dinner parties, ties and jackets are de rigeur for men and women should reserve jeans or trousers for sightseeing!

If invited to dinner, or to a home party, the invitation will usually be for a somewhat earlier hour than customary, e.g. in Britain. It is safe to add 30 minutes to the time specified by your host. Also, if you visit a family living in their own house, or in a block with its own garden, the chances are that you will be confronted with one or more dogs. Dogs in Hungary are not pets; they are at best burglar alarms and, at worst, potentially lethal weapons against intruders. Beware and wait for your host, or someone from his family, to take care of the beasts.

Unless you are on very intimate terms with the family, or it is made clear that the party is going to end very late, do not stay long after 10.00 pm, especially if the next day is a working day. People tend to get up early, dishwashers are relatively rare, and your hostess will want to face the next day fully rested!

Vörösmarty Square

4

Doing Business

Golden Eagle Pharmacy opened 1740

As in other situations, it is worth remembering, when doing business with your Hungarian hosts, that many of them have had their formative experiences in the Communist economy. Many of those you are likely to deal with, were educated by that regime. The older Hungarian businessman owes his present position as a businessman to having been an official of the Communist economic order. He will, therefore, tend to look over his shoulder much of the time, wary of being taken for a ride, but also of being stabbed in the back. He will need patience on your part, but he will have connections in banking, in all branches of business activity and also in a number of government departments. The young business-man will be well trained, very knowledgeable in the theoretical aspects of business and the economy and quick to learn the ropes of the market.

However, the thrusting, competitive char-acteristics of Western business and commercial life are only now being learnt in Hungary, and, it has to be said, sometimes manifest themselves in the least attractive forms of unrestricted, old-time capitalism, or, as it is styled in Hungarian, *untamed capitalism* (**vad-kapitalizmus**). Similarly, the skills for approach-ing the great international financial institutes and aid agencies with a view to raising capital for specific projects are still largely to be learnt. However, during the past five years, un-doubted advances have been made.

Hungarians are sometimes still surprised by the need for long and detailed agree-ments which British or American business partners demand; theirs is more a Continental European codified law which does not make it necessary to spell out all conditions of a contract and they will be dismayed by insistence on these.

On the whole, they tend to be tough negotiating partners and, as Hungarian currency (the Forint) is not yet fully convertible, will show an annoying insistence on Western partners covering the expenses of their business trips to the hard currency areas on joint business.

It is also worth noting that, while Hungarians as a nation are neither more, nor less honest than any other, they are not used to the 'my word is my bond' concept and will, as a matter of course, insist on written offers, tenders, agreements, confirmations. The telephone is for setting up an appointment, not to talk business, much less to make binding promises or to finalize agreements.

Secretarial and clerical training is still, after five years, lagging far behind what would be considered normal standards in Western Europe or North-America. Secretarial and clerical staff are pleasant and helpful, but, even the rare ones who can boast a working knowledge of a foreign language, are simply not used to the kind of efficiency level expected of a reasonably well-paid, and trained, secretary in London, Paris, Frankfurt, New York, or Sydney.

Although the service has improved out of recognition over the past five years, telephone communications in Hungary are still a different concept from what you are used to at home. This is only partly due to the network, which is one of the infrastructural areas named as top priority for investment, as to the lack of telephones in private home.

It is not unheard of for a businessman to be unreachable on the telephone in his home. More importantly, office workers tend to use the office telephones for their own urgent private calls during the first hour or two of the working day. That is when they call up their children's school, make appointments with dentists or hairdressers and invite friends to dinner. It is not uncommon to have to wait for your money at the cashiers' desk of a busy bank, while the cashier is nonchalantly talking with a friend about her holiday. Interruption will be resented.

With the privatization of MATA'V, Hungary's telecommunications giant, imminent, the extension of the infrastructure is only a matter of time. Consumers, however, deterred by inevitable price increases may not be quick to have telephones installed in their homes.

International Trade Centre

The Western, mainly American, habit of answering business letters on the telephone is alien in Hungary. All correspondence must be answered, letters with letters, fax with fax. Nor is it any more polite than in Western countries to telephone anyone in his own home on business, unless it is desperately urgent, or unless you are very friendly with the person concerned.

The business day begins early. Most offices, especially in the SME sector, tend to start at 8.00 am and close before 5.00 pm and, while the businessman may be willing to stay on as long as necessary for business, he will be unlikely to have much support from his staff after hours.

In government and local government offices, as well as business offices, office hours are 8.00 am to 4.30 pm (incidentally, times are almost always given in terms of the 24-hour clock, e.g. 0800–1630). You may call without an appointment between 9.30 and 12.00 noon. For visits before or after these times it is better to ask for an appointment.

These are the bank holidays of the Hungarian calendar:

1 January (New Year's Day)
15 March (National Holiday)
Easter Monday
Whit Monday
20 August (St Stephen's Day)
23 October (National Holiday)
Christmas Day
Boxing Day (which is simply called
    the second day of Christmas)

It is not customary for businesses to close down either for summer vacation, or for the days between Christmas and the New Year.

The business lunch is far rarer than in most Western countries, while business breakfasts are considered outlandish. The most common type of hospitality for the business visitor is coffee, at any time of the day or night. This almost invariably consists of minute cups of very strong espresso coffee which most Hungarians drink often, and without sweetener or milk. (Cream in coffee is unknown, with the exception of whipped cream on top of large cups of milky coffee, never seen in the world of business.) Any other business hospitality would normally be a reception, or a dinner invitation.

Business premises are not necessarily situated in office blocks, or buildings generally reserved for office use. Many Hungarian firms in the SME sector operate in ordinary flats in blocks of flats where perhaps all the other flats are occupied by families. Hence, as is the case with private addresses, the address of an office is not necessarily indicative of its creditworthiness, or its standing in its field of business activity.

Although much less often than before, lawyers also may have offices which form part of their homes, just as most doctors see their private patients in a surgery which is simply one of the rooms in their home. This is no reflection at all on their professional status or competence, it only indicates that they are either not partners in a larger law firm, or that they are considering you their private client.

5

Eating and Drinking

Marzipan confectionary shop in Párizs Street

The first word that comes to mind in this context is *caution* – because the food tends to be spicy and, very often, too heavy, or rich, for the West-European or North-American stomach. Spiciness comes, in the main, from a generous use of pepper and, especially, paprika. The richness comes from the cream, sour cream and, very often (especially in private households and more basic restaurants), pork fat which are frequently used in cooking. The tastes are good, but the price one may pay in wakeful nights and expanded waistlines may be exorbitant!

Your typical Hungarian hostess will not take no for an answer – certainly not the first 'no'. Most good guests demur at first, then give in to temptation for a second (indeed, third!) helping. Only the second or third 'no' is taken seriously, accompanied by the assurance that you loved the food, but simply cannot cope with more.

The meal begins with soup more often than not. While the concept of the cold (or even hot) *hors d'œuvre* is by no means alien to Hungarians, the variety of soups is great, and most of them are not considered less elegant, or attractive, than other kinds of first courses.

Probably the best known Hungarian dish is *gulyás*, the word meaning cowherd. However, unlike anywhere else in the world, this is, in fact, a soup. Its main ingredients are beef, cut into small cubes, paprika, tomato, green peppers, potatoes and a variety of green vegetables. It is, of course, a very filling soup and it is unwise to order any but the lightest of main dishes to follow it.

It is impossible to list all the dishes on the menu of a good Hungarian restaurant; but cold fruit soups (preferably in warm weather) stuffed cabbage or stuffed green peppers (*töltött káposzta, töltött paprika*) ought to be tried. Paprika chicken and paprika veal are general favourites and seldom assail the Western digestive organs seriously.

Hungarian wines are more varied than Western supermarkets would suggest. The most famous of all, however, *Tokaji*, is a fine but a very heavy dessert wine, similar to sherry, and not to be ordered *with* the meal. Beer in Hungary is constantly gaining in popularity and, as many British visitors have been pleased to discover, some of the Hungarian brews are excellent. Hungarian beer comes in two colours: *világos* (light) and *barna* (brown). The former is lager, the latter a malty stout. What all but the most died-in-the-wool teetotaller must try is *pálinka* (very strong brandy) which can be distilled from apricots (*barack*), pears (*körte*), cherries (*cseresznye*) or plums (*szilva*). A small measure of one of these before a meal may help to cope with spices and fat!

Street market

The cost of food, for visitors with Western currency, is still very reasonable, inflation notwithstanding and, while a few particularly elegant restaurants, especially in international hotels, may have much higher prices (although noticeably less than in most of Western Europe) it is still perfectly possible to have an excellent three-course meal with wine for as little as £5.00 ($8.00) per person.

Naturally, the more modest the establishment the less does it cater for foreign visitors. Hence, the food will be perhaps more genuine, but certainly less accommodating to foreign taste-buds and foreign digestions.

Should you find yourself in Eger (an important town and county seat in the north-east) or its neighbourhood, you should try one of the innumerable 'wine-cellars' (some of them are genuine wine cellars) for a wine-tasting meal. This usually consists of an array of cold meats, cheeses, a selection of pickles and breads, served with six, eight, or more varieties of wines, ranging from the driest, at the outset, to the sweetest at the end. A pleasant, if somewhat numbing, gastronomic experience.

6

Accommodation in Hungary

Fishermen's Bastion reflected in Budapest Hilton

Hungary is a popular tourist destination and the foreign visitor is well advised to book his accommodation in good time, especially between May and September.

As everywhere else, the types and prices of accommodation vary a great deal. The major international hotels in Budapest, such as the Atrium Hyatt, the Fórum Budapest, the Budapest Hilton and some others, offer accommodation and services (including business and conference services) of the highest standard and charge similar prices (normally set in US$ and D-Mark) to those charged by top-class hotels in Western Europe. Even second-line establishments charge well upwards of $100 per night.

The alternatives include marginally out-of-town hotels, some available on a self-catering basis, tourist hostels (very cheap but basic and far out of Budapest), camping and paying guest service. The latter may be compared to a British seaside bed-and-breakfast arrangement and the paying guests, while having their own room, sometimes have to share bathroom facilities with the hosts. Such accommodation is normally offered by elderly people living on their own in larger apartments. This is available for about £10.00–£15.00 ($16–$24) per night.

By far the best arrangement is to rent an apartment from 'absentee landlords' i.e. families away on holiday or business (a few landlords maintain an apartment for letting and live elsewhere). Here the snag is that these are not officially registered and therefore difficult to find.

Tourinform (361-117-9800 if dialled outside of Hungary) will provide information in English, German, or French.

7

Money, Shopping and Leisure

Zoological Gardens, Budapest

Hungary's currency is the **forint** and one **forint** contains 100 **fillérs** – the latter, however, may be safely ignored for practical purposes. The rate of exchange fluctuates – at the time of writing, between 190 and 200 to the £, 150 and 160 to the $. The government is gradually devaluing the Forint by about 12–15% altogether. This helps to keep Hungary still relatively cheap for the Western visitor.

The best known and most welcome foreign currencies are the US$ and the Deutschmark but Sterling is also very acceptable. In legitimate trade, however, foreign notes or coins are rarely accepted except in banks, hotels and money exchange shops (the latter being the most expensive way of changing your money or traveller's cheques). There is little to choose between these.

The advantage of the TC, apart from the obvious one of protecting the holder from financial loss if stolen or lost, is that Hungarian banks are fastidious with the physical condition of the note and refuse to accept ragged or even very slightly mutilated ones.

Payment by credit card is accepted only in international hotels (ask upon checking in), the best (and most expensive) restaurants and by a handful of luxury shops selling antiques, pieces of art or jewelry, although the habit is steadily spreading. American Express and Access are the most popular. IBUSZ the (tourist agency) also accepts VISA cards, the Budapest Bank welcomes the EUROCARD, and MASTERCARD is accepted by the Kereskedelmi Hitel Bank (Commercial Credit Bank) branches. As for TCs, never assume that they will be accepted in any shop or restaurant.

Banks are open for the public between 9.00 am and 1.00 pm. OTP (the bank which probably has the most branches and is the equivalent of the High Street bank, is open between 8.00 am and 4.00 pm (8.00 am – 6.00 pm on Mondays).

As in all countries, the shopper is best advised to shop away from obvious tourist traps (e.g. the Castle district or the pedestrian precincts of **Vörösmarty tér** and **Váci utca** and their immediate neighbourhood in the heart of the 'Inner City' of Budapest, or **Szentendre**, a lovely showpiece of a small town a half-hour train ride from the centre of Budapest). These, however, are the most likely places where the street vendor or the shopkeeper may speak some English or German.

Bargaining is absolutely unknown and unacceptable in shops. As for street vendors, those with stalls and the prices displayed will not accept bargaining, but the innumerable countrywomen plying their embroideries and other folk art objects (mostly genuine) will. On the whole, however, bargaining is not so generally accepted as in the East and there is little to gain from the trouble it takes.

Bargain hunters may be disappointed unless they wish to collect prints or drawings of Budapest scenes, or Hungarian folk-art pieces. However, leather goods are usually excellent value for money and so are books and records. An enormous selection of quality CDs are available at low prices and books are still extremely cheap compared with Western prices, despite the constant price rises. A fair number of books are available in foreign languages (especially in German and English) in most bookshops in the Inner City.

Opening times on weekdays are usually between 10.00 am and 6.00 pm except food shops which are open between 6.00 am

1845 etching of Chain Bridge, Budapest

and 8.00 pm. (Small food shops from 8.00 am to 6.00 pm.) Saturdays are strictly for morning shopping, with practically nothing open after 2.00 pm. Some major shopping centres and food shops, however, are also open on Sunday mornings. In most shops, except the one-man hole-in-the-wall, or the self-service stores (there are few of these), you are supposed to make your choice first and take a bill from an assistant, then pay at the cashier's and receive your goods wrapped against the stamped bill. In every shop where you may buy special presents, you can ask for your purchase to be gift-wrapped at no extra cost.

If you are an admirer, or collector, of Hungary's famous **Herend** china, it is worth paying a visit to the Herend shop (within a stone's throw of the Forum Hotel). This china is quite expensive, but cheaper there than any-where else and the selection is far wider. They also take orders for items not immediately available.

Leisure activities are fairly cheap and varied, although somewhat restrained by the language barrier which deprives the visitor of the enjoyment of usually good theatrical performances at prices that are a fraction of Western theatre ticket prices. Nor is the world of the cinema open, as most foreign films are dubbed.

Summer visitors would do well to exploit the great variety of swimming pools, both open-air and covered. Some are splendid, like the richly decorated art-nouveau pool in the Hotel Gellért with its statuary, green marble, potted plants and aerated water, others may go back to the time of the Turkish occupation in the seventeenth century.

Thermal baths of Gellért Hotel & Spa

The musical life of Budapest is as vigorous as it is varied with two opera houses and a number of excellent concert halls working through the season, and the open-air opera and concert performances throughout the summer season. Again, for the Western visitor, admission fees are small, although obtaining tickets may be difficult.

For the enterprising visitor who wishes to see more of the country in a relatively short time, day excursions from Budapest abound. Apart from the organized ones, on tourist coaches, which are mostly arranged by IBUSZ and advertized on leaflets in all hotels, it is not difficult to drive, or take a long-distance tram to places like Aquincum (not more than twenty minutes on the tram) which is a sizeable Roman relic in the vicinity of Budapest complete with a small but good museum and amphitheatre.

On the same road (or tram line) but farther out is Szentendre. Although something of a tourist trap, it has an extremely pleasant atmosphere, a number of excellent restaurants, interesting shops to browse in (all open on

Saturdays and Sundays), a number of pictur-esque and well-kept buildings and a few good museums. Situated on the Danube, it is also approachable by boat from Budapest.

Yet further, still in the same direction, but no longer on the tram line, are Visegrád and Esztergom. The first used to be the home of a number of medieval kings whose ruined palaces look down on the beautiful Danube bend from wooded hills. Not far from the ruins is the Sylvanus Restaurant with its special game dishes.

Esztergom is the Canterbury of Hungary – the see of the country's Roman Catholic primate. The Basilica dominates the scene and offers a magnificent view on the neighbouring hills, the Danube, and part of Slovakia across it. The town is small but picturesque, and has a few good museums. It may be of some interest to British visitors that an ancient chapel, restored in the 1970s, was dedicated, upon re-consecration, to Thomas à Becket (it had always been called the Thomas Chapel (*Tamás kápolna*).

The Lake Balaton, 70 km long, but hardly more than 3 km wide at its widest, is one of Hungary's beauty spots. It is easily reached by car within two hours. Probably its most picturesque spot is Tihany, built on a mountai-nous promontory, with its ancient Abbey.

Travelling Inside Hungary

Western Railway Station (1874–77)

Public transport, inflation and periodic fare revisions notwithstanding, is still reasonably inexpensive in Hungary. In Budapest, it consists of tramcars, buses, trolley buses and the underground system called Metro. Ticket costs are very reasonable (Ft. 35) and the same on any of these – regardless of the distance. However, as Budapest is a sprawling city and every time you change from one form of transport to another, or change buses, trams or trolley buses (on the Metro system you may, of course, transfer from one line to another with the same ticket) you need a new ticket, it is worth buying either blocks of 10 or more tickets, or weekly season-tickets (Ft. 720). The latter offers unlimited travel for several days, but must be accompanied by a card with your photo on it – valid for ten years!

Tickets can be bought at Metro stations and most tobacconist's or newspaper kiosks, but one must be careful always to have tickets *before* boarding. The pre-bought tickets must be validated for the journey. At Metro stations this is done by an automat placed before the down escalator. It clips off a corner of the ticket. On buses, trams and trolley buses the automat will punch holes in the ticket for validation. Inspectors make life uncomfortable for passengers without validated tickets.

Incidentally, locals who do not validate tickets are not all cheats; most inhabitants of Budapest have some sort of cheap season ticket available for OAPs, students, school-children, and full-time employees who work in the capital.

The Metro system is easily understood and offers quite a comprehensive service in and near the centre of Budapest. The trains are fast and frequent and the carriages clean.

Trams, buses and trolley buses are subject to delays caused by traffic jams and road works and are usually quite crowded but, generally, they provide a good service. It is customary for young people to give up their seats to the elderly, especially to older women passengers and you may still quite often see men offering their seats to younger women who, liberated as they may be, are quite willing to accept them.

Standing in queues is unknown at tram, bus or trolley bus stops. Boarding one of these

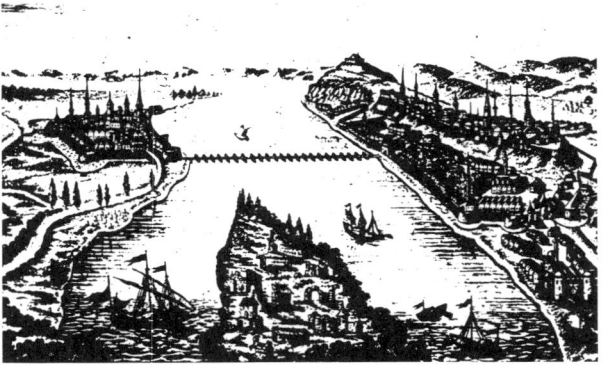

View of Pest and Buda (1602) during Turkish occupation

vehicles in peak hours is a total free-for-all. (Again, some mercy is shown towards older women, but everybody else is subject to the laws of the survival of the fittest.)

There are many taxis in Budapest and they are totally deregulated. Some are run as individual enterprises, most belong to larger firms, or cooperatives. They all must have a certified meter, however, and the wise passenger will not accept the offer of a lump-sum fare, for instance, from **Ferihegy Airport** to a hotel in the heart of Budapest but always insist on paying by the meter.

Long-distance travel (such as there is in a country where the farthest major city is 266 km, or about 160 miles, from the capital) can be done by car, long-distance bus, or the railways. At present, there are no internal flights in Hungary. Trains, with the exception of the newly installed Intercity trains which run between Budapest and a few major destinations, tend to be slow and fairly crowded. They are also subject to delays. Hungary, incidentally, suffered its first ever railway strike in April 1995, although the railway employees' union allowed some 'essential' trains (e.g. those

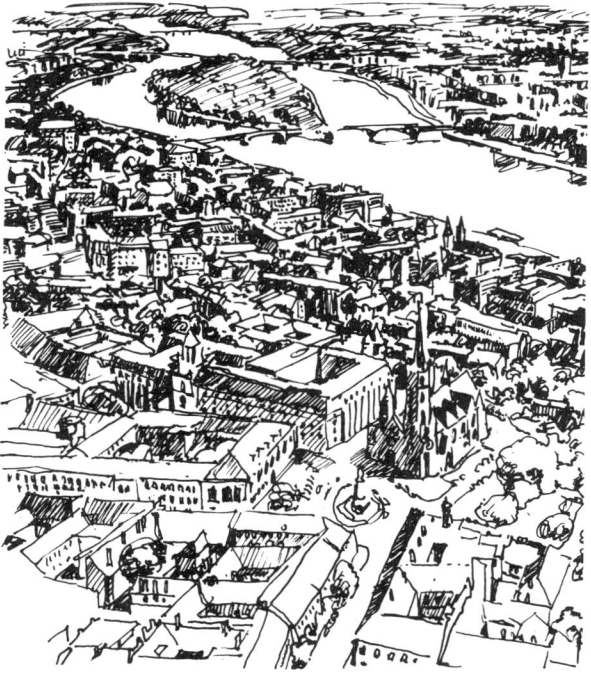

View of the Danube at Magit Island

transporting food supplies to Budapest, or international express trains) to operate.

Budapest has three major railway terminals: **Nyugati pályaudvar** (= *Western Station*) which is the oldest and has the distinction of having been built by Eiffel of Eiffel Tower fame, **Keleti pályaudvar** (= *Eastern Station*) from which most international trains leave and **Déli pályaudvar** (= *Southern Station*) which is the most modern one and from which it is possible to travel to the **Lake Balaton**, Hungary's Riviera, as well as to some foreign destinations to the South or South-West of Hungary. The railway stations are all connected by the Metro system.

Both **Nyugati** and **Keleti pályaudvar** have foreign currency exchange offices which operate on a 24-hour basis.

Parking in Budapest, although liberal by any Western standard, is still extremely difficult in the city centre. Road signs are only concerned with long-distance driving and give no help to the driver who wants to find different parts of the city. The Hungarian Automobile Club runs a breakdown service. Details of this can be obtained at frontier crossing points.

The telephone number of the Budapest municipal breakdown service is 252–2800. Motorists must remember that the legal limit of alcohol in blood is 0.08 – i.e. practically 0. Speed limits are 120 km/h (70 mph) on motorways, 100 km/h (60 mph) on motor roads (the equivalent of A roads), 80 km/h on all other highways and 60 km/h (36 mph) in built-up areas. Motorcyclists must wear crash-helmets and use a dimmed headlight even in daylight hours. The only EU countries from which Green Card international insurance cover is required are France, Greece and Italy.

Faiths and Politics

Detail from Franz Joseph (Liberty) Bridge

Among religious faiths and affiliations, Christianity is predominant in Hungary, with nearly 88% of the population having been baptised into one of the Christian churches and denominations. Roman Catholicism claims just over 64%, while Protestants comprise more than 23% of the nation. The most important non-Christian religion is Judaism but, owing to the Holocaust and subsequent Jewish emigration, less than 1% of Hungarians are practising Jews.

Very few Hungarians have kept faith with Marxism after the collapse of the Communist state. Six main parties emerged from the collapse:

AFD (Hungarian: SZDSZ)	–	Alliance of Free Democrats
AYD (Hungarian: FIDESZ)	–	Alliance of Young Democrats
CDPP (Hungarian: KDPP)	–	Christian Democratic People's Party
HDF (Hungarian: MDF)	–	Hungarian Democratic Forum
HSP (Hungarian: MSZP)	–	Hungarian Socialist Party
ISP (Hungarian: FKGP)	–	Independent Smallholders Party

The first free elections took place in May 1990 and ended with the rout of the Communists. A coalition government led by the MDF took over with the CDPP and the ISP as junior partners. This Centre Right government soon found that – even though the last years of the Communist regime saw a number of much needed economic reforms half-heartedly carried out, or at least launched – a reversal of the damage caused by four decades of ideological command economy was far beyond its strength.

This, combined with what many people perceived as incompetence, high-handedness and corruption in government circles, produced a partial reversal of fortunes among the parties in the 1994 general elections. The HSP (essentially the rump of the former ruling Communist Party) achieved a spectacular landslide victory. Although constitutionally capable of forming a government of its own, the HSP opted for coalition with the AFD.

The present state of the parties in Hungary's unicameral parliament is as follows:

GOVERNING COALITION		OPPOSITION	
HSP	209	HDF	38
AFD	69	ISHP	25
		CDPP	22
		AYD	20
		Indep.	3
	278		108

The May 1994 electoral landslide is best illustrated by the fact that the Hungarian Socialist Party had around 30 mandates in the previous parliament! However, a significant reversal of fortunes was observed already in the autumn of 1994 when, in the local government elections, the government parties lost a lot of ground. This was mainly due to local agreements between opposition parties to withdraw less likely candidates in favour of those from one or the other opposition party if they looked more likely to be successful.

The 1994 general election did not affect the presidency as the president is elected for a term of five years. The current President of the Republic is Mr Arpád Göncz (AFD).

The new, Centre Left government set out to turn the economy, at present battling against a nearly 20% rate of inflation, a foreign indebtedness which stands at about the same level as during the last months of the Communist regime ($28bn plus), and over 10% unemployment, with an economic reform package consisting of devaluation, savage cost-cutting and speedier privatization – hardly a socialist ideology-inspired programme.

While the tough economic policies of the socialist Gyula Horn's new coalition government have predictably eroded much of its popularity, supporters of the government point to its unassailably strong position in Parliament and hope that the economy may be turned round before the campaign for the next election (due in 1998) begins. Opponents of the government pin their hopes on an emerging anti-socialist alliance of the HDF, CDPP and AYD which, with the absence of the former extreme right wing of the HDF, and the presence of AYD, may offer a viable centrist alternative.

Hungary's basic foreign-policy objective of joining NATO and the EU at the earliest possible date remained unaffected by the change of government. The country has been trying to mend fences with its most antagonistic neighbours, the Slovak Republic and Romania, both with very large Hungarian ethnic minorities whose minority rights the present Hungarian government, similarly to its predecessor, considers as its legitimate concern. To promote friendlier relations, 'Framework Agreements' have been signed with both countries, but relations, especially with the Slovak Republic, have hardly improved.

The military conflict in the former Yugoslavia is also a constant source of worry, with large numbers of refugees (many ethnic Hungarians among them) in Hungary. It may be said that, of all Hungary's neighbours with important Hungarian minorities within their borders, relations are best with the Ukraine. (Ethnic Hungarians living in Austria's Burgenland are fewer in number and are generally content to consider themselves Austrians.)

Hungary is an ethnically monolithic country, with over 96% of its population Magyar. The only ethnic minority which attracts adverse prejudice are the Gypsies (often referred to as Roma) who speak a mixture of Hungarian and Romany, and whose culture and way of life differ most from those of the rest of the population. While efforts at 'affirmative action' are made to rehabilitate them, and integrate them with the rest of the population, this meets with opposition not only from Magyars but, increasingly, from leaders of the Roma community as well who wish to be considered as a national minority with its separate identity.

Count Jósef Eötvös (1813–71), culture minister

10

The Language

The Hungarian language is not a member of the Indo-European family and, therefore, it has little in common with any Romance, Germanic or Slavic language. The only nation-state where a similar (i.e. Finno-Ugrian) language is spoken is Finland, but the similarity is meaningful only for the trained linguist.

The spelling of Hungarian is phonetic which means that, with very few exceptions, all sounds are transcribed with precisely the same letters or groups of letters (unlike *there-their*, *mail-male*, *read-reed* etc.). There are no prepositions, these being replaced by suffixes, which makes the noun change its form quite often. (E.g. *the table* = **az asztal**; *on the table* = **az asztalon**; *to the table* = **az asztalhoz** etc.) Another characteristic of Hungarian is vocal harmony: all suffixes and verb endings have two or three versions because high and low vowels cannot mix. (E.g. **asztal<u>on</u>** [*on the* *table*] but: **széken** [*on the chair*] *because* **é** *is a high vowel, while* **a** *is low.*

These elements, combined with a fairly difficult conjugation of verbs, make Hungarian a hard language to learn and, of course, no attempt is made here to teach it. On the other hand, Hungarian is made somewhat easier by the fact that it is a unisex language: it lacks genders. There are no separate pronouns for males and females. The articles (**a** and **az**) simply reflect whether the word begins with a vowel or a consonant; <u>az</u> **asztal**, but <u>a</u> **szék**.

Another Hungarian characteristic is that the predicate of a sentence may not be a verb. (E.g. **Meleg a leves** = *the soup is hot*. In this brief sentence there is no equivalent of the verb *is*; the adjective **meleg** = *hot* is enough.) This, together with the fact that the ending of a verb makes the use of the pronoun unnecessary (e.g. **megyek** = *I* go) and that another ending also replaces the possessive pronoun (e.g. **anya** = *mother*, **anyám** = *my mother*) tends to make the language concise. (**Megyek anyámhoz** = *I am going to my mother*.)

Like most people who speak a little-known language, Hungarians are very pleased if their foreign visitor bothers to learn a few polite words or phrases, such as the following:

USEFUL WORDS AND PHRASES

Jó reggelt	*(yow reghelt)*	Good morning; hello
Jó napot	*(yow nopot)*	Good day; hello
Jó estét	*(yow ashtait)*	Good evening; hello

Jó éjszakát	*(yow aisokaht)*	Good night
Viszontlátásra	*(visontlahtahshro)*	Good bye (verbatim: so long)
Köszönöm	*(kuhsuhnuhm)*	Thank you
Szívesen	*(seeveshen)*	My pleasure
Hogy van?	*(hodj von)*	How are you?
Köszönöm, jól	*(kuhsuhnuhm, yowl)*	Very well, thank you (in reply to the above)
Jó étvágyat	*(yow aitvahdjot)*	Good appetite (customary before all meals)
Foglaljon helyet	*(foglolyon heyyet)*	Please, take a seat
Örvendek	*(uhrvendek)*	Pleased to meet you
Nagyon sajnálom	*(nodjon shoynahlom)*	I am very sorry
Bocsánat	*(bochahnot)*	Excuse me
Szabad	*(sobod)*	May I?

THESE SIGNS MAY BE USEFUL:

Nem bejárat	*(nem beyahrot)*	No admission
Kijárat	*(kiyahrot)*	Exit
Vészkijárat	*(vaiskiyahrot)*	Fire (emergency) exit
Zárva	*(zahrvo)*	Closed
Nyitva	*(nyeetvo;* **ny** *as* **gn** *in cognac)*	Open
Vigyázatl	*(vidjahzot)*	Danger!
Dohányozni tilos	*(dohahnyoznee tilosh)*	No smoking
Pénztár	*(painstahr)*	Booking office; Cashier

Gyógyszertár *(djowdjsertahr)*		Dispensing chemists
Patika	*(potiko)*	[as above]
Étterem	*(aitterem)*	Dining room; Restaurant
Orvos	*(orvosh)*	Doctor
Fogorvos	*(fogorvosh)*	Dentist
Kórház	*(kowrhahz)*	Hospital
Rendörség	*(renduhrshaig)*	Police
Foglalt	*(foglolt)*	Reserved; occupied

DAYS OF THE WEEK:

Hétfo	*(haitfuh)*	Monday
Kedd	*(kedd)*	Tuesday
Szerda	*(serdo)*	Wednesday
Csütörtök	*(chytuhrtuhk)*	Thursday
Péntek	*(paintek)*	Friday
Szombat	*(sombot)*	Saturday
Vasárnap	*(voshahrnop)*	Sunday

NUMBERS:

egy	*(edj)*	one
ketto	*(kettuh)*	two
három	*(hahrom)*	three
négy	*(naidj)*	four
öt	*(uht)*	five
hat	*(hot)*	six
hét	*(hait)*	seven
nyolc	*(nyolts)*	eight
kilenc	*(kilents)*	nine
tíz	*(teez)*	ten

húsz	*(hoosse)*	twenty
harminc	*(hormints)*	thirty
negyven	*(nedjven)*	forty
ötven	*(uhtven)*	fifty
hatvan	*(hotvon)*	sixty
hetven	*(hetven)*	seventy
nyolcvan	*(nyoltsvon)*	eighty
kilencven	*(kilentsven)*	ninety
száz	*(sahz)*	hundred
ezer	*(ezer)*	thousand

11

Did You Know ... ?

View of Danube and Chain Bridge built 1849

Hungary is one of the few countries in the world with a negative population growth. (It is −0.1%)

The population of Hungary is 10.3 million of which 2 million live in the capital, Budapest.

In 1991, 36 million arrivals by foreign nationals were registered at Hungary's border-crossing points and air terminals. In proportion, this is like some 200 million people arriving in Britain in one year.

Latin was Hungary's official language of administration until the third decade of the nineteenth century.

The first permanent bridge to span the Danube in Hungary was Budapest's **Chain Bridge** designed by Adam Clark. It was based on the pattern of the old Hammersmith Bridge, London, built by Clark and now crossing the Thames at Marlow. The square at the Buda end of the bridge is named after Adam Clark.

In proportion to its population, Hungary's Olympic competitors have won more gold medals since the 1936 Games than any other country in the world.

Although a landlocked country, Hungary has a merchant fleet of 17 vessels totalling a deadweight tonnage of nearly 143,000.

Following the suppression by the Soviet Army of the Hungarian national uprising of October-November 1956, some 200,000 refugees left the country to settle abroad.

The oldest line of the Budapest Metro was the first underground railway line built in Continental Europe.

In 1996, Hungary will celebrate its 1100th birthday as a nation state.

Ethnic Hungarians in Romania constitute the largest national minority in Europe.

Hungary's per capita GDP was the third highest in Eastern Europe in 1993, after Slovenia and the Czech Republic.

River Pest and international hotels